KT-394-222

CONTENTS

ANCIENT SPORT

OLYMPIC OLDIES

Sport goes back into ancient history. We have no idea whether prehistoric people played sport, but who knows? Perhaps they raced each other to the nearest warm cave or played catch with the skulls of their enemies!

The first organised sporting event that we know of is the Olympics, which first began in ancient Greece around 776 BCE.

Running in the nude The main event was a sprint of around 200m (656ft) in length. The male athletes ran it naked, their bodies smeared with olive oil and dusted with fine sand, to protect them from sunburn.

First flame The Games were held in honour of Zeus, the king of the gods. At the beginning of the Olympics a flame was lit at Zeus's altar, just like the stadium torch at the modern Olympics.

Naked Greek runners took part in the early Olympics.

Soldiering as sport Those who took part in the armour-wearing race had to run carrying over 25kg (55lb) of ancient Greek military kit, including a helmet, leg-pieces and a shield.

Serious scrapping In ancient Olympic boxing, fighters wore leather thongs wrapped round their hands, with menacing pieces of sharp metal fixed on their knuckles.

SPORT!

MOIRA BUTTERFIELD

W
FRANKLIN WATTS
LONDON•SYDNEY

Weird True Facts! the boring stuff...

This edition published 2014 by Franklin Watts

Copyright © Franklin Watts 2014
Franklin Watts
338 Euston Road
London NW1 3BH

Franklin Watts Australia
Level 17/207 Kent Street
Sydney, NSW 2000
All rights reserved.

A CIP catalogue record for this book
is available from the British Library.

Dewey no: 796

ISBN: 978 1 4451 2970 9

Printed in China.

Franklin Watts is a division of Hachette Children's Books, an Hachette UK company

www.hachette.co.uk

Series editor: Sarah Ridley
Editor in Chief: John C. Miles
Designer: www.rawshock.co.uk/Jason Anscomb
Art director: Jonathan Hair
Picture research: Diana Morris

Picture credits: AFP/Getty Images: 11b, 17t.age footstock/Superstock: 7t.
Fadi Al-Assaad/Reuters/Corbis: 14b.Steve Allen/Dreamstime: 28t. David Allio/Icon SMI/Corbis:
23c. John Angerson/Rex Features: 24b. Chris Arend/Getty Images: 9b. Bettmann/Corbis: 7b.
Mark Blinch/Reuters/Corbis: 13tl. Adrian Brown/Alamy: 9tl.
B. Calkins/Shutterstock: 28b. Christophe Dupont/Elise/Corbis: 21t. Epicstock Media/Shutterstock:
26t. Explorer Media Pty Ltd Sport the Library/Dreamstime: 20b. Flashstudio/Shutterstock: 19c. Paul
Gapper/Alamy: 15b. Robert Hallom/Rex Features: front cover tr. Stan Honda/AFP/Getty Images:
25b. Hulton Archive/Getty Images: 11tr. Imageworks/Topfoto: 10t. Keystone-USA/Rex Features:
front cover tl. Douglas Kirkland/Corbis: 19t. Pornchai Kittiwongsalud/AFP/Getty Images: 15t. KVA-
SAY/Shutterstock: 6. Peter Macdiarmid/Getty Images: 8bl. David Madison/Getty Images: 29b.
MARKA/Alamy: 22b. Nagy Melinda/Shutterstock: 23t.Tim Moran/Rex Features: 27tl. NASA: 27b.
Alexander Naturskin/Reuters/Corbis: 14t. Jean-Erick Pasquier/gammarapho/Getty Images: 17b.
Petitfrere/Dreamstime: front cover b, 16. Planetpix/Alamy: 13b. Adam Pretty/Getty Images: 11tl.
Quirky China News /Rex Features: 21b. renkshot/Shutterstock: 29t. Rex Features: front cover c,
27tr. Moses Ribinson/WireImages/Getty Images: 29c. Taina G. Rissanen/WireImage/Getty
Images: 24t. Chico Sanchez/Aurora Photos/Alamy: 18t. Alistair Scott/Shutterstock: 8br.
Sipa Press/Rex Features: front cover cr, 26b. Sportgraphic/Shutterstock: 19b. Wolfgang Thleme/
epa/Corbis: 23b. Mark Thompson/Getty Images: 13tr. Topfoto: 10b.Tony Tremblay/istockphoto:
20t. Friedeman Vogel/Getty Images: 12.Emma Wood/Alamy: 8t. World History Archive/Alamy:
18b, 22t. Theo Zierock/AFP/Getty Images: 25t. Zurbagan/Shutterstock: 9tr.

*Every attempt has been made to clear copyright. Should there be any
inadvertent omission please apply to the publisher for rectification.*

SPORT!

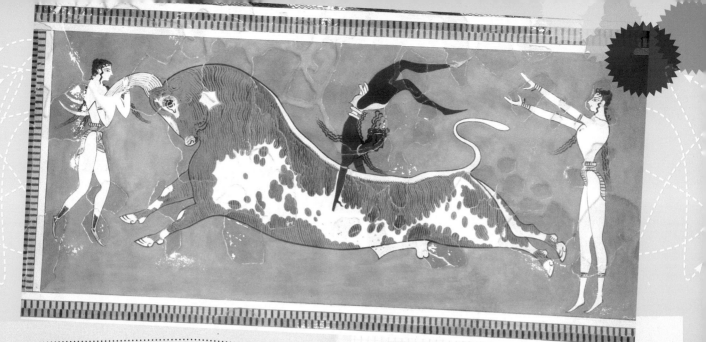

Loopy sports from long ago

Some ancient sports sound very dangerous…

This wall painting shows the mysterious Minoan sport of bull-jumping.

Don't try this at home Around 1700 BCE, on the Mediterranean island of Crete, the ancient Minoan people made wall paintings and sculptures showing young men leaping over a charging bull, grasping it by the horns and doing a back flip over the top of it. This mysterious sport has been given the name 'bull-jumping'.

Sizzling strength test The Shaolin monk-warriors of ancient China had a very unusual weightlifting sport – red-hot cauldron-lifting. This test of strength and mind-power for the super-tough monks left them branded for life by the patterns etched on the metal cauldron. The skin marks were seen as a sign of worthiness.

When they began

Some of today's popular sports go back a long way, but be warned. Sporting origins often cause lots of arguments!

A type of hockey was played in ancient Egypt. Players used a ball made from scrunched-up papyrus leaves, and sticks carved from wood.

In medieval Europe whole villages and towns played football, with few rules. The contests could be so violent that some rulers tried to ban them.

A version of football played in Florence, Italy, in the 1600s, in a giant sandpit laid out in the middle of town.

WE'VE ALWAYS DONE IT THIS WAY!

Some modern sports events are steeped in tradition going back hundreds of years. In some cases everyone's forgotten how they started in the first place…

World championship shin-kicking at the Cotswold Olimpicks.

The Ouch Olimpicks The Cotswold Olimpicks started in Chipping Campden, Gloucestershire, UK, in 1612 and they are still being held 400 years later. Among the events is the World Championship shin-kicking contest. Contestants try to kick their opponent's shins to make them fall over.

Xtreme cheese-chasing Every May, a crowd of contestants race down a very steep hill near Cheltenham, UK, running after rolling cheeses. The event may derive from very ancient midsummer ceremonies, but no one is sure. Because the hill is so steep the cheeses roll very fast, making injuries common among the cheese-chasers.

A schwingen time Schwingen is a special type of Swiss wrestling dating back to the 1200s at least. Contestants wear a sacking loincloth over their ordinary clothes, and the first wrestler to throw his opponent wins. At Switzerland's biggest Schwingen festival, the prize for the champion is a bull.

Contestants tumble downhill after a rolling cheese, in Cheltenham, risking injury for cheesy victory.

A Swiss Schwingen contest, in which competitors wear sacking loincloths.

The sport that always comes back The sport of boomerang-throwing originated in Australia, where for centuries the Aborigine People used the curved stick for hunting. Now there are world championships, with events including long-distance throwing, juggling and catching.

A boomerang decorated with Aboriginal painting.

Wanna fight with a kite? Kite-fighting has long been a national sport in Afghanistan, and is also played in India and southeast Asia. The fighting kites are fitted with tough string coated with crushed glass, and the aim is to cut your opponent's string so that their kite falls out of the sky.

This person is taking part in the Inuit version of trampolining.

Snowy sports

Inuit People from the far north sometimes meet up for sporting contests. Here are some traditional Inuit sports:

Blanket bounce Players jump on a walrus- or seal-skin blanket held up by others. It's based on an old hunting technique, when a hunter bounced high to spot far-off animals.

Back-pushing A competitor sits on the floor back-to-back with his opponent, with arms interlocked. The aim is to push your opponent backwards.

Toe-jumping Competitors take off their shoes, squat down and grasp their toes. They try to jump forwards, without letting go of their toes. The winner is the one who jumps the furthest and lands balanced.

WHILE THE WORLD WATCHES

The world's biggest sporting events are not immune from crazy happenings, this time played out in front of millions.

The 1904 Olympic marathon on a dusty road near St. Louis, USA. The winner secretly hitched a lift.

CHEATING BIG-TIME

Every four years the Summer and Winter Olympics are watched on TV by billions. The winners become world-famous, so perhaps it's not surprising that they occasionally cheat.

The first cheats Bribery and cheating took place in the ancient Olympics thousands of years ago. Offenders were fined and their money used to pay for a statue of Zeus with their name on it. The statues of shame were then put on display for everyone to see.

Runners go wrong In 1904 US Olympic marathon winner Fred Lorz was about to get his gold medal when officials discovered he had secretly hitched a lift in a car for 17km (11 miles) of the race.

DOPEY DOPERS

World-renowned sportspeople are regularly caught using drugs to enhance their performance in major events. Here are just a few of the most unusual occurrences:

The first Olympic athlete to fail a drug test was Swedish pentathlete Hans-Gunnar Liljenwall. In 1968 he tested positive for beer.

Swede Hans-Gunnar Liljenwall (left) drank beer to steady his nerves, and so became the first Olympic drug test failure.

Olympic horse Waterford Crystal was given a banned substance by his rider.

In 2004 show-jumping gold-medal-winning horse Waterford Crystal became the first Olympic animal to test positive for drugs.

Michel Pollentier (seated) was caught providing someone else's urine for a drugs test.

Catch that cup

The FIFA World Cup is watched by over a billion people in countries all over the world. The gold cup itself, called the Jules Rimet Trophy, has had an unusual history.

In 1966, just before the World Cup was held in the UK, the cup was stolen from an exhibition in London. It was later found under a hedge by a dog called Pickles, out for a walk with his owner.

The trophy was stolen again in 1983 when it was on display in Brazil, inside a case with a bulletproof front. Thieves simply broke into the back of the case and fled with the cup, which has never been found.

In 1978 Michel Pollentier was disqualified from the world's top cycle race, the Tour de France, when he gave a fake urine sample for drugs-testing. He had a system of tubes hidden under his shirt, to pump someone else's urine from a hidden container.

ENTER TODAY!

To be a world sporting champion you usually need to train for long hours and be unusually talented, but here are some world championships where less dedicated sportspeople might just stand a chance…

Messy, weird and fun — mud-covered competitors take part in the European Mud Olympics.

Get messy

The **European Mud Olympics** are held every year near Hamburg in Germany. Over 500 contestants take part in mud-caked events, including mud football, mud volleyball, tug-of-war, fish tennis and an eel relay race using fake eels made from inner tubes filled with rotting fish innards.

Swamp soccer is played in muddy bogs or deliberately-flooded pitches. The soggy sport began in Finland as a tough training exercise for soldiers, and now there are around 260 swamp soccer teams around the world.

Every August in Wales, UK, competitors vie for the title of **World Champion Bog Snorkeller** by swimming through a water-filled trench in a

Contestants at the Rock-Paper-Scissors World Championships. The pirate won.

YOU COULD BE CHAMPION!

The **Rock-Paper-Scissors (RPS) World Championships** are held every year in Toronto, Canada, and the winner gets a huge cash prize. Experts who run the event insist that this is a game of skill and cunning.

The **World Kissing Competition**, held in Italy, hosts events such as 'underwater kissing' and 'basketball kissing'. Meanwhile the endurance kissing record was smashed by a Thai couple in a 2011 World Championship event, when they kissed for 46 hours and 24 minutes.

The **World Conker Championships** are held in Northamptonshire, UK, every year. Players (above) compete with conkers gathered from horse chestnut trees, threaded on the end of string. They must swing their conker, trying to smash their opponent's nut into pieces.

The **Summer Redneck Games** are held every year in Georgia, USA. Anyone can enter events such as 'the mud pit belly flop' (above), the 'seed spitting contest' and 'bobbin' for pig's feet'. There's also toilet-seat throwing, hubcap hurling and an armpit serenade competition.

Some world championship rules to remember

Swamp soccer: There is no offside rule because nobody can see the pitch markings.

Kissing: No sitting or sleeping. Referees must accompany kissers to the toilet.

Mud pit belly flop: The winner makes the biggest splash.

13

ANIMALS WELCOME

Animals take part in mainstream sports such as horse racing and show-jumping, but these animal events definitely fall into the 'unusual' category.

Piglets chase a football covered in fish oil at the Pig Olympics.

The Pig Olympics

In the Pig Olympics, organised by the Sport-Pig Federation, piglets from different countries compete in running, swimming and pigball (football). In 5-a-side pigball matches, the piglets chase a ball coated in tasty fish oil to attract them. They must push it over the goal line with their snouts.

CRITTER RACING

Camel-racing has been popular in Middle Eastern countries for many years but, controversially, small children were once used as jockeys. Now robot jockeys are fitted to the camels instead.

Queensland, Australia, is the home of some unusual animal racing. Cane toads, cockroaches and lizards all have their own Queensland racing championships.

Every year, on Christmas Eve, dogs take part in the Scotland Island 500, a 500m (1,640ft) swim off the coast of Sydney, Australia. The prize is a bowl inscribed with the words 'Outstanding Canine Aquatic Behaviour'.

A robot jockey on board a racing camel.

DREAM TEAM

Here are some examples of animals and humans coming together in the name of exciting sport.

Elephant polo Played in India and Sri Lanka, the rules of elephant polo are similar to horse polo, but two people ride on each elephant – a player and an elephant trainer.

Polo-playing elephants chase a ball and try not to step on it!

Worm-charming The World Worm Charming Championships are held every year in Willaston, Cheshire, UK. Competitors are given a small plot of land and must try to encourage worms to the surface in a given time, using vibrations and music. The world record is 567 worms charmed up from one plot.

Worm-charmers try to tempt worms up during the World Worm Charming Championships.

Top five weird animal sports

1 Camel-wrestling is very popular in parts of Turkey and an annual championship is held in Selcuk.

2 Otis the dog had a special sky-diving harness and dived in tandem with his owner, wearing doggles (goggles for dogs).

3 In rabbit show-jumping, trained rabbits jump over mini fences in a ring.

4 In Asian countries the sport of insect-fighting draws crowds of gamblers. Stag and rhino beetles, pumped up with sugarcane, are popular as fighters.

5 Oriental Roller pigeons are brilliant aerial acrobats, and this has led to the sport of pigeon acrobatics.

STRONG STUFF

Sports that rely on strength and fighting are amongst the oldest in history, and they're still very popular worldwide. Here are some lesser-known examples…

Weird wrestling

Head heats Goanna-pulling is an Australian tug-of-war sport between two competitors facing each other on all fours, connected by a heavy leather strap round their heads. They are said to look like goanna lizards, hence the name of the sport.

Toe to toe The World Toe Wrestling Championship is held every year in the UK, and organisers even applied, unsuccessfully, to get the sport into the Olympics. Contestants interlock their big toes and try to push over their opponent's foot. The referee starts a bout by shouting 'toes away'.

Slippery tradition Oil-wrestling is a national sport in Turkey. The festival held at Kirkpinar every year has been going since 1357. Competitors cover themselves in olive oil and wear special knee-length calfskin breeches called *kisbet*. Contests can be won by achieving an unshakeable hold on the kisbet.

Turkish oil-wrestlers covered in olive oil, wearing their special kisbet trousers.

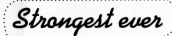
Strongest ever

Every year super-strong body-builders compete for the title of the World's Strongest Man. The competitors build up a points tally by taking part in all sorts of different events, including:

ANVIL-DRAGGING,

PULLING A TRUCK,

CARRYING TWO FRIDGE FREEZERS,

GIANT LOG LIFTING,

CAR CARRYING.

Karl Fokan of South Africa attempts the truck pull in the 2005 World's Strongest Man competition.

Top five strange strength and fighting sports

1 In chessboxing players alternate between rounds of speed chess and boxing. A contest can be won either by a boxing knockout or a chess checkmate.

2 Ear-pulling is a traditional Inuit sport. Players sit facing each other, joined by a strap looped around an ear. The contestants pull apart until the loop falls off or somebody gives in.

3 In an Inuit ear weight contest competitors lift lead ingots attached to their ears by lengths of twine.

4 Leg-wrestling, also called Indian Wrestling, begins on the floor, where contestants lie down opposite each other and interlock a leg. They push until one of the players flips over.

5 All around the world there are different types of traditional wrestling, called folk wrestling. In Mongolian Boke wrestling, for instance, fighters wear short jackets, boots and tight briefs.

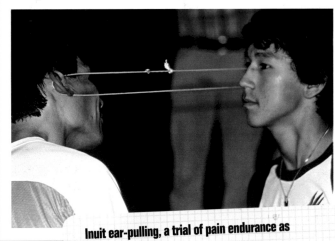

Inuit ear-pulling, a trial of pain endurance as much as strength.

SOME ARE WEIRDER THAN OTHERS!

Every sport needs some rules to ensure a winner, and sometimes a referee to make contests go smoothly. Here are a selection of unusual sporting rules and amazing referee stories.

WIN OR DIE

The Mesoamerican Ballgame was played around 3,500 years ago by the Mayan communities of Central America. Crowds lined ball courts to watch players try to get a heavy rubber ball into a wall-mounted hoop, without using their hands or feet. This all sounds like fun, but Mayan carvings show losing team captains being sacrificed to the gods after the game.

A reconstruction of the Mayan ballgame, without the ritual sacrifice of the losing captain.

The ancient Olympic sport of pankration was a violent mixture of wrestling and boxing. Players weren't allowed to gouge eyes or bite, but they could do anything else. Victory was by a knockout, submission or death. One three-time champion, Arrichion of Phigalia, won his final title when he was already dead. He expired moments after his opponent gave in.

The ancient Greek pankration made modern cage-fighting look soft.

Competitors get messy during a cherry pie eating contest in Idaho, USA.

Strangest sporting rules

No mess, no sick During competitive eating championships, competitors, called 'gurgitators', must abide by strict rules. In some contests, eaters are not allowed to 'chipmunk' – to store food in their cheeks. A 'reversal' (vomiting) means instant disqualification. You can find out more about competitive eating events on page 25.

Get a grip if you get a goal World football rule-makers FIFA have banned 'excessive goal celebration'. Players can be sent off for taking their shirt off, making gestures at the crowd or doing cartwheels after scoring.

This football player could get booked for 'excessive celebration'.

Referee!

Head case In 2011 an Australian Rules football referee took the unusual decision to send off a player because his hair was too dangerous. Nathan Van Someren of the Simpson Tigers had to leave the field in case his mohican hairstyle poked another player in the eye.

A lot of bottle In 2011 a drunken referee started sending off players at random during a Czech football league match. The sozzled ref had come straight from a party, and stumbled around the pitch falling over.

RACING WITH A DIFFERENCE

Racing is probably the easiest sporting concept to understand, but that doesn't mean it can't be made weird, or very, very hard to do!

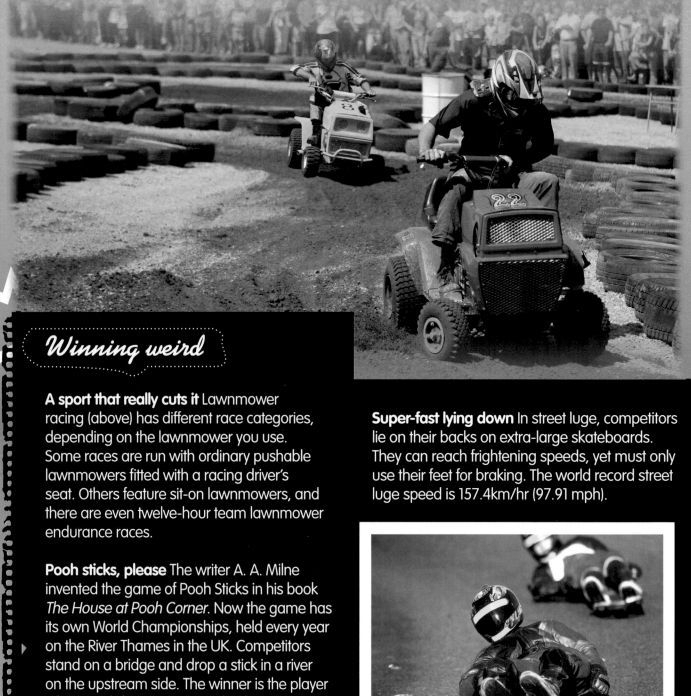

Winning weird

A sport that really cuts it Lawnmower racing (above) has different race categories, depending on the lawnmower you use. Some races are run with ordinary pushable lawnmowers fitted with a racing driver's seat. Others feature sit-on lawnmowers, and there are even twelve-hour team lawnmower endurance races.

Pooh sticks, please The writer A. A. Milne invented the game of Pooh Sticks in his book *The House at Pooh Corner*. Now the game has its own World Championships, held every year on the River Thames in the UK. Competitors stand on a bridge and drop a stick in a river on the upstream side. The winner is the player whose stick first appears under the other side of the bridge.

Super-fast lying down In street luge, competitors lie on their backs on extra-large skateboards. They can reach frightening speeds, yet must only use their feet for braking. The world record street luge speed is 157.4km/hr (97.91 mph).

Superfast and no brakes… street lugers put their backs into it.

HARDEST RACES EVER

These races sound like they need a lot of training…

Racing with balls Joggling is the sport of running while juggling. At the Joggling World Championships, held in the USA, races include 3-, 5- and 7-ball juggling, and club juggling, too. Any juggler who drops a ball must go back to the place where the drop occurred and begin again.

Only for the toughest The hardest running race in the world is the Marathon de Sables, which is held over six days through the Sahara Desert in Morocco. It's the equivalent of running six ordinary marathons, day after day.

On the up The sport of stair climbing, or tower racing, has its own World Cup ranking system. Athletes take part in events around the world, racing up the stairs in skyscrapers and towers, to gain points. One of the toughest is Sears Tower in Chicago, with 2,109 steps. Top competitors complete it in around thirteen minutes.

The Marathon de Sables, for fitness nuts only.

Competitors take part in the 1,975 step stair race in Chongqing, China, in 2010.

MOTORISED MAYHEM

Racing is perfect for machines with wheels, and makes for some exciting and unusual sporting events.

The first ever official car race, held in Paris in 1894.

CRAZY CARS

It starts with steam The first ever car race was held in 1894 between Paris and Rouen. It was advertised as a 'Competition for Horseless Carriages'. The first car over the line was driven by Count Jules-Albert de Dion, but it was disqualified because it was a steam car, not a petrol car, and needed a stoker to refill its boiler as it drove along.

The greatest adventure The 1907 Peking-Paris Race is seen by many as the greatest long-distance car race ever. Five cars took part and had lots of extraordinary adventures, including falling through wooden bridges, getting stuck in quicksand and being rescued by locals. After months of driving, four of the cars finally made it to Paris.

Still going strong The Le Mans 24-hour race has taken place since 1923 and is the oldest endurance race in the world. Three-man teams compete, taking it in turns to drive round the French circuit for a day and a night.

Wot, no satnav? A competitor in the 1907 Peking-Paris Race uses a local guide to find the way.

Extreme motorsport

The US Monster Jam series pits giant custom-built pick-up trucks against each other in thrilling races and freestyle events. The monster trucks have huge wheels up to 1.67m (5ft 6in) tall, and are built for short bursts of speed up to 161km/hr (100mph). They can even fly through the air.

Top fuel dragsters are the fastest racing vehicles in the world. They can accelerate from 0–160km/hr (0–100mph) on 0.7 seconds, and reach speeds over 480km/hr (300mph) during their short but super-fast runs. Races only last for around 4 seconds.

A custom-built SUV easily drives over a scrap car during a Monster Jam event in the United States.

Flames shoot from a top fuel dragster as it streaks forward.

Cycle ball players score a goal using their brakeless bicycles.

Weirdest wheel sports

Chainsaw wars Hand-held power tools are adapted and pitted against each other in power tool drag racing. Belt sanders, angle grinders, chainsaws and drills race against each other along wooden tracks.

Cycle scoring Cycle ball is played by teams of two riders. Players are not allowed to put their feet on the ground as they ride round a court on brakeless bikes, trying to score a goal.

CRAZY COMPETITIONS

These sports rely on contestants with particularly unusual skills. Some might say craziness is one of them…

This wife-carrier is using the popular 'Estonian Carry' technique to transport his Missus.

All in the family

The World Wife-Carrying Championships take place every year in Finland. According to locals, it's a tradition from centuries ago, when outlaws regularly stole women from local villages. Competitors from all over the world carry wives along a course with obstacles to climb over and a water jump to wade through.

• The wife doesn't have to be the carrier's own.

• Dropping a wife incurs a 15-second penalty.

• Wives must weigh a minimum of 49kg (108lb) or carry a weighted rucksack.

• The winner wins his wife's weight in beer.

FACE IT

Gurning is officially 'the sport of contorted face-making'. The World Championships are held every year in the UK, and prizes are awarded to the ugliest contortion. Contestants are judged by how much they can transform themselves, so a naturally ugly person doesn't have any advantage.

Four-times World Champion Peter Jackman was so dedicated to the sport he had his teeth removed to make his face more flexible.

An entry in the 2001 World Gurning Championships, which took place in Egremont, Cumbria.

GIANTS OF EATING

Competitive eating is popular in the USA and Japan, and draws big TV audiences. The International Federation of Competitive Eating organises the major league events, the most important ones being contests in hot-dog, pizza and hamburger eating. Contestants win by eating the most food in a given time.

The US Nathan's Hot Dog eating contest. Contest winners can eat over 60 dogs and buns in 10 minutes.

SOME OFFICIAL FOOD RECORDS:

47 slices of pizza in 10 minutes

3.8kg (8.4lb) baked beans in 2 minutes 47 seconds

2.26kg (5lb) birthday cake in 11 minutes 26 seconds

2.49kg (5.5lb) buffet food in 12 minutes

2.72kg (6lb) cabbage in 9 minutes

4.98kg (11lb) cheesecake in 9 minutes

Chewing champions

US competitor Sonya Thomas is the world's top food-eating star, with more than twenty world records.

Joey Chestnut is another famous food-eating name, and is the repeat winner of the top hot-dog-eating contest. He has held many world eating records, including eating 7.5 litres (2 gallons) of chilli con carne in 6 minutes.

Sonya Thomas on her way to a turkey-eating world championship.

25

ON THE EDGE

Some sportspeople revel in extreme challenges that seem far too dangerous, or too daft, for the rest of us.

Professional surfer Billy Kemper rides a giant wave in Maui, Hawaii, on 13 March 2011.

Watery ways to be extreme

Catching a monster Giant wave surfers go questing around the world to catch gigantic waves, which tend to build up quite far offshore. They are towed out to possible wave sites by jet ski, and risk their lives riding walls of water the size of buildings.

Breathtaking sport Freedivers don't wear scuba tanks but rely on their ability to hold their breath as they dive. It's a very risky sport that requires a lot of training. The breath-holding record for men is over 11 minutes and for women it's over 8 minutes.

EXTREMES ON LAND

Crazy climbing Free soloing is an extremely dangerous form of climbing in which the climber uses no safety equipment at all. It needs intense concentration and strength, and has led to a number of deaths.

Sky sport Skydiving has developed some extreme versions, including freestyle dancing while freefalling, and 'base-jumping' – parachuting from fixed objects such as buildings and bridges. In wingsuit flying, participants wear a suit that turns them into a human glider.

Russian extreme sports athlete Valery Rozov performing a wingsail jump in Queen Maud Land, Antarctica.

THE WEIRDEST EXTREME SPORT EVER?

Extreme ironing is a combination of tough outdoor pursuits, such as rock-climbing or skiing, and ironing. It even has its own championship, with events including ironing up a tree or in a fast-flowing river.

An extreme ironer gets the ironing done on a car journey.

Extreme ironers show off their ironing prowess underwater.

Extreme places to play

Seasick soccer The football team on the small Norwegian island of Utsira was very successful, winning all its home matches, until referees realised that the team had an unfair advantage. Getting to the island by boat means sailing across rough sea, leaving visiting teams horribly seasick. Now Utsira have to play all their games away.

Space sports In 1971 US astronaut Alan Shepard hit the first golf shots on the Moon, and in 2011 Japanese astronaut Satoshi Furukawa carried on the hobby of space sport by playing baseball on the International Space Station. Thanks to weightlessness he was able to pitch to himself, then float round and hit the shot, and then catch himself out.

Alan Shepard drives a golf ball on the Moon. He said it went for 'miles and miles and miles'.

WEIRD AND WONDERFUL EQUIPMENT

Sportspeople need all kinds of special equipment, but here is some equipment you might not find down at your local sports shop.

A Scottish caber-tosser about to chuck his giant log at a Highland Games.

"Excuse me. Do you stock…?"

Dynamite If you want to play Tejo, a national sport in Columbia, you'll need some small paper packets filled with dynamite and dotted around a central target in a box. Points are gained by players throwing a metal disk (the tejo), to explode the packets and land in the target.

A giant tree trunk In the Scottish sport of caber-tossing, contestants throw a long tree trunk around 5.94m (19.5ft) long, and weighing 79kg (175lb). Judges award prizes according to distance and throwing style.

Animal ankle bones At the Naadam Festival in Mongolia, crowds watch anklebone shooting teams flicking sheep, goat, horse or camel bones at targets along a wooden board. Mongolian leader Ghengis Khan is said to have invented the sport to strengthen the middle fingers of his archers.

A handful of horseshoes The sport of horseshoe-tossing is competitively organised across the USA by the National Horseshoe Pitchers Association. Players throw horseshoe-shaped pieces of metal at stakes arranged in a sandbox track.

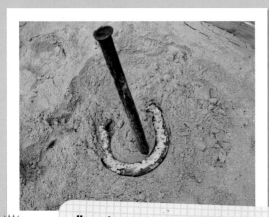

Horseshoe - tossing is played competitively across the USA.

A Formula One racing car is the most expensive piece of sports equipment in the world.

WORLD'S MOST EXPENSIVE

If you have $50,000 (£32,000) to spare, you could buy a pair of diamond-encrusted Nike trainers, but these sparkling shoes aren't the most expensive sports equipment ever. The cost of building and running a Formula One motor racing car has been estimated at £4.76 million, making it the world's costliest piece of sporting equipment.

Rapper Big Boi holds one of the diamond-encrusted Nike trainers at an event in 2007.

World's richest

If you want to afford those diamond trainers, you need to become a golfer, a basketball star, a tennis ace or a Formula One driver. These are the top-earning sports stars in the world, easily led by the golfers.

US golfer Tiger Woods is at the top of the money charts, earning $62 million a year in 2011.

GLOSSARY AND WEBSITES

Ancestors Relatives from long ago.

Base jumping Parachute jumping from fixed objects such as towers or bridges.

Blanket tossing Inuit sport of jumping high on a walrus-skin blanket held by people below.

Bog snorkelling An event where competitors swim through a water-filled muddy trench.

Boomerang Traditional Australian curved stick once used in hunting, now used in a throwing sport.

Buildering Climbing buildings.

Bull-jumping Ancient sport of back-flipping over the top of a charging bull.

Caber-tossing Scottish sport of throwing a large tree trunk.

Chipmunking Storing food in the cheeks during a food-eating competition.

Chessboxing A contest that mixes chess and boxing rounds.

Cotswold Olimpicks Games held in the UK since 1612, including World Championship shin-kicking.

Cycle ball Sport where cyclists try to score a goal on a pitch, whilst never putting their feet on the floor.

Doping Taking illegal performance-enhancing drugs to get better sporting results.

Dragster A racing car adapted to go very fast over a very short distance.

Ear-pulling An Alaskan Inuit sport whereby two players pull on string looped between their ears.

Elephant polo Polo played from the back of elephants.

FIFA The Fédération Internationale de Football Association, soccer's world governing body.

FIFA World Cup The soccer world cup. There are events for both men and women.

Folk wrestling Traditional forms of wrestling played in specific countries.

Formula One A category of motor racing sport.

Freediving The sport of diving without wearing air tanks.

Free soloing The extreme sport of climbing with no safety equipment.

Goanna-pulling Australian sport in which two players pull on a strap looped between their heads.

Gurgitator A contestant in a food-eating competition.

Gurning Competitive face-pulling.

Inuits Tribal people of the far north, who have their own traditional sports events and games.

Joggling Running while juggling.

Jules Rimet Trophy The cup awarded at the end of the men's soccer World Cup.

Kite-fighting Sport in which kite flyers try to cut the strings of their kite-flying opponents.

Marathon de Sables Tough 6-day running race held in the Sahara Desert.

Mesoamerican Ballgame (also called the Mayan ballgame). A ballgame played 3,500 years ago in Central America. Losing players could be sacrificed.

Minoan Ancient civilisation on the island of Crete, where bull-jumping took place.

Mud Olympics Games held in Germany every year, where all the events are played in mud.

Muktuk-eating Whale blubber eating contest.

Oil-wrestling A popular Turkish sport in which contestants cover themselves in olive oil before fighting.

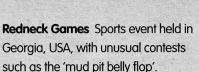

Olympics An international event including many sports. First begun in ancient Greek times.

Oriental Roller A type of pigeon. Owners enter the pigeons in acrobatic events.

Pankration A violent ancient Greek mixture of boxing and wrestling.

Performance-enhancing drugs: Chemicals that alter the body to make a sports competitor perform better.

Pigball Five-a-side piglet soccer. The ball is coated with fish oil to encourage the piglets to snuffle at it.

Pooh Sticks Game created by author A. A. Milne, played by racing two sticks under a bridge.

Redneck Games Sports event held in Georgia, USA, with unusual contests such as the 'mud pit belly flop'.

Reversal Being sick in a food-eating competition.

RPS Rock-paper-scissors game, also sometimes called 'Scissors, paper, stone'.

Scotland Island 500 A sea swimming race for dogs, held in Sydney, Australia.

Shaolin monks Monk-warriors of ancient China, who developed martial arts.

Schwingen Traditional Swiss wrestling.

Skydiving Jumping from a plane and freefalling before opening a parachute.

WEIRD SPORTS WEBSITES

http://www.worldrps.com/
The World Rock-Paper-Scissors Society, organisers of the world championships, give tips on winning your games.

http://www.boomerangsrus.com/
boomerang-throwing-tips.htm
How to throw a boomerang successfully.

http://www.wormcharming.com/
Learn about worm-charming and see a photo gallery of the World Championships.

http://www.ballgame.org/main.asp?section=3
Learn all about the Mesoamerican Ballgame, where losers were sacrificed, and join in an interactive version of the game to see if you would survive.

Note to parents and teachers

INDEX